THE color GARDEN

(yellow)

THE color GARDEN

(yellow)

single color plantings
for dramatic landscapes

TEXT & PHOTOGRAPHY BY ELVIN MCDONALD
INTRODUCTION BY BRIDE M. WHELAN

CollinsPublishersSanFrancisco
A Division of HarperCollins*Publishers*

A Packaged Goods Incorporated Book

First published 1995 by
Collins Publishers San Francisco
1160 Battery Street
San Francisco, CA 94111-1213

Conceived and produced by
Packaged Goods Incorporated
9 Murray Street, New York, NY 10007
A Quarto Company

Design by Stephen Fay
Endpapers by Michael Levine
Series Editor: Kristen Schilo

Seeds © Copyright 1995 White Swan Ltd., Beaverton, OR. White Swan® and Garden Accents® are registered trademarks of White Swan Ltd.

McDonald, Elvin.
　　The color garden (yellow) : single color plantings for dramatic landscapes / text & photographs by Elvin McDonald.
　　　　p.　　cm.
　　Includes Index.
　　ISBN 0-00-225080-2
　　1. Yellow gardens.　　I. Title.
SB454.3.C64M39 1995
635.9'68—dc20
　　　　　　　　　　　　　　　　94-37910
　　　　　　　　　　　　　　　　CIP

Color separations by Wellmak Printing Press Limited
Printed and bound in Hong Kong by Sing Cheong Printing Co. Ltd.

10 9 8 7 6 5 4 3 2 1

yellow's
for shining lights
and angels
Bonny and David
Larry and Lea
Janis B.
Betsy K.

Thanks to the gardens and gardeners who permitted me to photograph...

Barnsley House Gardens, England; John Brookes and Denman's Gardens, England; Brooklyn Botanic Garden, Brooklyn, NY; Francis Cabot, La Malbaie, Quebec; The Chelsea Flower Show, London; The Conservatory Gardens, Central Park, New York City; Descanso Gardens, La Canada Flintridge, CA; Great Dixter Gardens, England; C.Z. Guest, Palm Beach, FL; Hidcote Manor Garden, near Broadway, England; Hortus Bulborum, Heiloo, The Netherlands; Jasmine Hill Gardens, Montgomery, AL; Royal Botanical Gardens at Kew, London; Leonardslee Gardens, England; Lilypons Water Gardens, Brookshire, TX; Longwood Gardens, Kennett Square, PA; Meadowbrook Farms, Meadowbrook, PA; Mercer Arboretum & Botanic Gardens, Humble, TX; University of Minnesota Landscape Arboretum, Chanhassen; Moody Gardens, Galveston, TX; Museum of Garden History, Lambeth Church, London; National Wildflower Research Center, Austin, TX; The New York Botanical Garden, Bronx, NY; Old Westbury Gardens, Old Westbury, NY; Planting Fields Arboretum, Oyster Bay, NY; Plum Creek Farm, Sharon, CT; Sissinghurst Castle Gardens, England; Strybing Arboretum, San Francisco, CA; Upton House Gardens, England; Wakehurst Gardens, England; William Wheeler, New York City.

Rudbeckia fulgida 'Goldsturm' is a cultivated form of black-eyed-Susan with black-cone centers and saturated yellow ray flowers.

contents

introduction

*W*ith yellow-orange and orange on its warm side and yellow-green and green on its cool side, yellow creates an array of endlessly moving patterns as well as dazzling shocks of color. This vibrant hue carries the eye from one section of the garden to the other in an orderly flow, much like a musical score. The yellow garden is active. It is spontaneous, joyous, and warm.

Yellow is the first hue of early spring. The harsh browns of winter are lonely and unfriendly. Then, in April, the yellow crocus bursts onto the landscape with astonishing contrast. Likewise, the yellow-green leaves of the willow tree, silhouetted against the gray spring sky are resplendent in their sway and lift the spirit.

Yellow's summer season begins with the showy brilliance of

the low marigold. The flaming orange and yellow daylilies of June (*pages 36 and 39*); July's warm and sturdy zinnias; and finally, August and September's dusky orange California poppies (*page 38*) are all major players in the movement through the yellow palette.

The medium wavelength of definable color is yellow. As light is radiant, visible energy, those flowers reflecting the color yellow are the ultimate expressions of significant brightness and movement. To better understand yellow, think of the circular sun and moon. The circular brilliance of the yellow garden excites, rather than providing a place of comfort and repose. In a yellow-hued garden it is important for the eye to experience an occasional restful space. A dominant yellow garden is best as a walk-through garden with intersecting and divergent pathways, slicing through the yellow and harnessing its constant sense of movement.

The natural opposite of yellow on the color wheel is violet or purple. The violet of the early spring crocus and variegated pansies, combined with the jutting iris, establish a perfect seasonal complement that does not impair or clash with the visual brilliance of yellows, such as lantana and gold coleus. The violets create a natural boundary in which yellow is controlled, allowing the eye to come to rest naturally.

BRIDE M. WHELAN

(I)

b e d s   a n d   b o r d e r s

*Y*ELLOW IS FOR THE SUN. ITS RADIANCE IS THE GARDEN'S LIFE source. Through the centuries various yellow daisy flowers have been called "marigold," for Mary's gold, presumably the Virgin Mary. The Old World pot-marigold *(above)*, *Calendula officinalis*, flowers in cool but frost-free sunny weather, in any expression of yellow, from pale cream to dark orange. The New World marigolds, developed from *Tagetes* native to Mexico, are choice for warm days— tiny-flowered, fern-leaved Signet types used as edgers in a strolling garden *(left)*, or any of a variety from knee- to chest-height, with flowers the size of large oranges.

Universally, loyalty and honor are associated with yellow. In the Northern Hemisphere the spring month of April is considered yellow; summer, yellow and blue; the fall month of September, orange or gold; and autumn, gold and brown.

Persian buttercups, the
Ranunculus of florists,
bloom in spring from tubers
set the previous fall. Besides
purest yellow (above), they
come also in white, orange,
red, and pink.
Swatches of yellow pansies
(Viola) interspersed with
tall snapdragons
(Antirrhinum) in a formula
mixture that includes bright
yellow help celebrate the
season around a classic
water lily pool.

Surely one of the noblest yellows of the spring season is the peony, a bit surprising since the flower itself is so often equated with the ultimate in floral pinks, roses, reds, and whites.

One of the earliest flowering is the central Caucasus herbaceous species *P. mlokosewitschii*, with large, single, lemon-yellow flowers carried above tidy, knee-high clumps of bluish-green leaves.

The tree peony species *P. lutea* from western China represents the class of peonies referred to as the "King of Flowers" in China and the "Flower of Prosperity" in Japan. First brought to the West in the late eighteenth century by Sir Joseph Banks, to the Royal Botanical Gardens at Kew, London, a preponderance of today's yellow tree peony hybrids are from American breeder Dr. A.P. Saunders. His cultivars include 'Age of Gold,' 'Canary,' 'Golden Bowl,' 'Golden Mandarin,' 'Golden Vanitie,' 'Gold Finch,' 'Gold Sovereign,' 'Roman Gold,' and 'Silver Sails' (palest yellow).

The herbaceous peony *Paeonia sterniana* (above, left) is a yellow-flowered species from southeast Tibet. The tree peony species *P. lutea* and cultivars (above, right) are among the spring border's most treasured yellow flowers for garden show and for cutting to bring indoors.

Paeonia mlokosewitschii, a yellow herbaceous species, highlights spring in "Mrs. Winthrop's Garden," an area at Hidcote Manor Garden, Gloucestershire, England. Named for the mother of the original owner, it features mostly yellow and blue.

Goldenrod is an American native wildflower that has been much improved through cultivation and the crossing, deliberate or by chance, of several species of *Solidago*. Named cultivars range from compact bushes barely knee-high to tall ones shoulder-height that need staking. Outstanding for golden yellow late summer and fall. Best in full-sun.

Goldenrod species and cultivars of *Solidago* *(opposite page)*, *Telekia speciosa (left, upper)*, and *Achillea filipendulina* 'Coronation Gold' *(left, lower)* are all hardy perennial members of the daisy family that bring an abundance of yellow to beds and borders early summer through fall.

Based on a widespread misunderstanding, the goldenrod is falsely accused of causing allergies. Its big clusters of tiny yellow flowers are laden with pollen, but the grains are too heavy to fly. The troublemaker is the pandemic ragweed whose inconspicuous flowers fiendishly release pollen light enough to be carried by the slightest breeze.

Telekia's leaves are mostly at the base of the plant, so that the distinctive yellow daisy flowers stand out boldly. This perennial from southeastern Europe to the south of Russia may bloom the first year from seeds.

The achilleas offer a treasure chest of different yellows, from creamy to deep gold on ferny-leaved plants that hug the ground or can grow up to waist-high. Late spring to midsummer is their time; sunny, dry climates favor healthier leaves.

Golden variegated hakone grass (*Hakonechloa macra* 'Aureola') turns its most vivid yellow in a balance of direct sun and shade.

The ornamental grasses include several with yellow or golden leaves, *Hakonechloa macra* 'Aureola' or golden variegated hakone grass being one of the most obvious. It grows close to the ground, the lightly green-streaked leaves arching over each other in the manner of overlapping shingles.

Two varieties of the popular *Miscanthus sinensis* are distinctively—and similarly—cross-banded with evenly spaced yellow markings along the leaves, the main differences being that porcupine grass (*M.s.* var. *strictus*) is upright and more cold-tolerant than the more lax zebra grass (*M.s.* 'Zebrinus'). The best view of them is early or late in the day with back or cross lighting.

Other yellow grasses or grass-like plants: *Acorus gramineus* 'Ogon' (golden variegated sweet flag), *Alopecurus pratensis* var. *aureus* (yellow foxtail), and *Carex elata* 'Bowles Golden' (a sedge).

Zebra grass, *Miscanthus sinensis* 'Zebrinus' *(opposite)*, with gracefully arching yellow-banded leaves, and the similar porcupine grass, *M. s.* var. *strictus*, with spikier, more upright leaves, are best appreciated by watching as wind currents set in motion their sun and shade patterns. Porcupine grass is winter hardy into deep cold; both grasses can take the heat in sun and well-drained soil.

🌿 *Laburnum* x *watereri* 'Vossii' is an outstanding yellow-flowered tree for small gardens. It is most famous for training over an arbored walkway so that the yellow flowers through mid-spring show off to their best advantage, such as in the Queen's Garden *(right)* at Kew Gardens, London. Inside, the theme is pure gold; beds immediately outside the arbor bloom at the same time with English bluebells *(Hyacinthoides)*.

Shrubs having yellow leaves can stand out in beds and borders the same as flowers. There are numerous euonymus with evergreen leaves variously edged, margined, or colored entirely with yellow, from creamy to vivid; some can be almost too assertive in the landscape unless deftly mixed with yellow flowers or counter-balanced by bright to deep blues and blue-green leaves.

A yellow-variegated English holly *(Ilex)* trimmed to cone shape stands at the center of Tradescant's Garden *(left, upper)*, behind Lambeth Church in London, emphasizing the yellow blooms of *Inula* and *Asphodelus* and complementing the blue of German iris. The holly leaves also play up the pale green of the boxwood *(Buxus)* hedges.

California privet *(Ligustrum ovalifolium)* and its variety 'Aureum,' golden privet, are sometimes planted together and sheared into topiaries like this globe in a Japanese garden *(left, middle)*, or into bicolored hedging, sheared or informal.

'Goldflame' *Spiraea japonica* is a twiggy small shrub that is coppery early in spring, then bright, glowing yellow-green at tulip time *(left, lower)*, followed by a covering of pink flowers. Prune when they fade, removing entirely the oldest wood and the dead blooms from the strong young branches.

Large-flowered hybrid roses such as the grandiflora 'Gold Medal' *(left)* and the hybrid tea 'King's Ransom' *(below),* along with the smaller, cluster-flowered 'Goldilocks,' a floribunda, are a reliable source of glowing yellow—and rose scent— from the first blooms of summer until frost.

*T*he Austrian briar or Austrian yellow rose, *Rosa foetida*, brought to the West from Asia by the 16th century, has played an important role in the development of the yellow rose, climbers like the one trained on a brick cottage wall *(opposite, upper)*, as well as shrub and bush types. The double-flowered *R.f. persiana* (Persian yellow rose), crossed with a red-flowered hybrid perpetual seedling in 1900, produced 'Soleil d'Or,' the first large-flowered modern hybrid tea that was yellow.

Another yellow species variety, *R. banksiae* 'Lutea,' the yellow Lady Banks rose *(opposite, lower)*, is a thornless Chinese evergreen that puts forth one burst of spring bloom in milder climates. There is also the hardier, shrubbier *R.* x *harisonii*, or Harison's Yellow. The very recent English rose 'Graham Thomas' is everblooming, soft yellow, fragrant.

(2)

w a t e r   g a r d e n

*I*F EVER SUNBEAMS DANCE IN A GARDEN, IT IS WHEN THE PALE lemon water lilies *(Nymphaea)* are blooming *(opposite)*, or the creamy sacred lotus blossom *(Nelumbo)*, having risen up from a seemingly mucky grave, stands above undulating, curving leaves, radiant in the shimmering light. As the flower begins to age, the bold, primitive seed receptacle appears *(above)*. This juxtapositon emphasizes the contrast between the ephemeral petals and leaves and the life-giving, edible seeds that also perpetuate the plant.

There are many yellow-flowered plants suited to water gardening. Water lily and lotus grow from pots of earth submerged in a pond or pool, with the roots and lower plant parts underwater. The water poppy *(Hydrocleys nymphoides)*, grows on the water surface with lemon-yellow flowers, brown stamens, and a light scent.

Besides the grass-like flax lily *(Phormium)*, which has spikes of bright yellow flowers in warm climates and thrives in the constantly moist but drained soil of a pond or stream bank, there are also some grass-like plants with yellow leaves for setting in similarly wet spots: golden variegated sweet flag *(Acorus gramineus* 'Ogon') and golden sedge *(Carex elata* 'Bowles Golden'). Yellow or golden true grasses for planting in close proximity to water are golden ribbon grass *(Phalaris arundinacea* 'Luteo-Picta') and creamy yellow-striped giant reed grass *(Phragmites australis* 'Variegatus').

Plants that grow wild in boggy or swampy ground can sometimes make bold statements in the yellow garden. An aroid called skunk cabbage *(Lysichiton americanum)*, for the smell of its flowers and the plant's appearance, is widely adapted to temperatures. It grows in wet-to-moist humusy soil, leafing out and flowering in spring before companion plants interfere, especially the appearance of leaves on deciduous trees and shrubs, which change the "cabbage" plant's sunny spring warmth to cool summer shade. Besides the handsome leaves, the boat-shaped, pale-to-bright-yellow spathe part of the blossom is large enough to be appreciated at some distance. The 'Aurea' form of creeping Jenny, *Lysimachia nummularia*, is a suitable gold-leaved companion.

Grass-like flax lilies *(Phormium)* grow on a mild-climate pond bank *(above)* where the roots have a constant water source but conditions are not always boggy.

Lysichiton americanum (opposite), for temperate to subtropical bogs or swamp gardens, has pale yellow, boat-shaped spathes in the spring.

🍃 The marsh marigold (*Caltha palustris*) is suited to planting in boggy ground or up to a hand's width deep in water. Bright yellow buttercup-like flowers appear in spring. A double-flowered form, 'Flore Pleno,' has graced gardens since the 17th century.

The yellow water flag, *Iris pseuda-corus (right),* originally from Europe and North Africa, is cultivated in gardens over most of the world. It has also successfully colonized many wet sites—ditches, swamps, pond and stream banks—and is one of the tougher plants that produces showy yellow flowers every spring and early summer without fail. Deadheading after bloom will keep self-sown seedlings from becoming a nuisance. There is also a yellow-and-green-leaved form, 'Variegata,' that is most dramatic in spring.

Suited to similarly wet or boggy ground are the Louisiana iris such as 'Charlie's Marite' (pale yellow), 'Dixie Deb' (yellow), 'Dural Gold' (golden yellow), 'Fading Beauty' (strong yellow, fading to pale), 'Joy Flight' (yellow with lime veining), and 'Sun Dream' (non-fading light yellow). These elegant flowers and relatively graceful, grassy, clump- or colony-forming plants are suited to climates where winter cold is neither extreme nor protracted.

(3)

s p r i n g   y e l l o w s

*A*T NO TIME IS YELLOW SO MUCH APPRECIATED AS WHEN IT appears at the beginning of spring, thereby signaling the end of a dark, cold, even dreary time, and the dawning of an exuberant, expansive season. Golden crocus and green-ruffed yellow buttercup-like winter aconite *(Eranthis)* are harbingers that come out in winter at the merest hint of spring, to be followed by major players: primroses *(Primula)* from greenish- to reddish-yellow *(above)* and tulips *(Tulipa)* from the small yellow-and-white species *T. tarda* to the regal Darwin such as 'Golden Apeldoorn' *(opposite)*.

Perhaps no yellow of spring is more coveted than that of a bright golden, fragrant daffodil *(Narcissus)* such as 'King Alfred' or 'Unsurpassable.' The genus is as rich in garden yellows for spring as *Hemerocallis* (daylily) is for summer.

Scotch broom (*Cytisus scoparius*) has about as much gold in its gene bank as any spring-flowering shrub. Some are so richly saturated the color can be blinding on a sunny day. The paler to lemon-yellow selections *(opposite, upper)* have more subtlety for small gardens; they can look their best in mixed company with a strong yellow tulip such as the lily-flowered 'West Point' or the green-stitched, frilled and shirred 'Yellow Parrot.'

Basket-of-gold alyssum *(opposite, lower,* with white perennial candytuft, *Iberis sempervirens)*, like Scotch broom, can vary from rich egg-yolk yellow to paler lemon shades, the latter more easily worked into a theme of pastels for a spring rock garden or wall planting. Ordinary basket-of-gold *(Aurinia saxatilis)*, can be toned down by placing it next to spring whites such as candytuft, arabis, *Anemone blanda*, and Roman *Hyacinthus*.

Other herbaceous perennial spring yellows include Celandine poppy *(Stylophorum)*, for partly shaded, wild plantings and leopard's bane *(Doronicum)*, for pointing up yellow, blue, or white bulbs. *Corydalis, Chiastophyllum*, and selected *Cheiranthus, Erysimum*, and *Viola* can be the source for more spring yellows, especially for rock gardens, rock walls, massing by steps, and at the front of taller plantings, and for mixing or matching in pots.

The fabled orange crown imperial immortalized in Flemish paintings by the Dutch masters is also available in varieties having yellow bell flowers, such as *Fritillaria imperialis* 'Lutea maxima' *(above)* and the western American native *F. pudica* or yellow bell. These bulbs are for temperate gardens and spring blooms. Swift drainage is needed and dry soil in summer.

Corylopsis, a small genus of shrubs from Japan, blooms early, before its leaves come out. They, the witch hazels (*Hamamelis*), and the unusual *Stachyurus*, are among the season's earliest yellow flowers. The Cornelian cherry, *Cornus mas*, is another, a sturdy, self-reliant shrub that can grow into a tidy tree.

Trees for spring include weeping willows for yellow effect, yellow magnolias such as 'Elizabeth,' and the golden chain (*Laburnum*). Gardeners in warm regions can also grow fragrant, puffy, golden acacias, golden trumpet tree (*Tabebuia*), and yellow bells (*Tecoma*).

Yellow foliage is also another source for this color in the spring landscape. In addition to the previously mentioned *Euonymus* and the gold-variegated forms of holly (*Ilex*) there is the golden-leaved Japanese maple (*Acer japonicum* 'Aureum'), such oaks as *Quercus borealis* 'Aurea' and *Gleditsia triacanthos* 'Sunburst,' a honey locust with delicate, ferny leaves which are golden yellow at first.

🌱 *Corylopsis pauciflora*, the buttercup winter hazel (*above*, with 'King Alfred' daffodils), is one of several that blooms at the very beginning of spring, before it leaves. Greenish bracts hold the sweetly scented yellow flowers of *C. spicata*.

🐟 A golden oak of garden origin, *Quercus borealis* 'Aurea' (*opposite*), lights up a rainy day.

(4)

summer and autumn golds

𝓨ELLOW SUMMER FLOWERS HOLD ON TO THEIR COLOR EVEN in brilliant light. Among annuals the *Helianthus* sunflowers *(above)* are favored for garden show and cutting. Foremost among perennials are yellow daylilies *(opposite)* available in thousands of different cultivars. Their botanical genus is *Hemerocallis,* whose genes predispose yellow, gold, and orange; their genius lies with breeders who have coaxed from them every color in the floral rainbow— including white—except clear blue. By the cooler days of autumn, most of the garden's yellows will have deepened to gold, a warm color found in chrysanthe- mum, marigold *(Tagetes),* pot-marigold *(Calendula),* and *Rudbeckia* daisies.

🐦 The narrow-leaf zinnia (*Z. angustiflora* or *linearis*) comes in yellow, gold, and white varieties. It can be summer ground cover in sun or permitted to scramble over the side of a window box. It tolerates long, hot summers and needs little care.

🐦 California poppies (*Eschscholzia*) in their native state are usually this color, a soft orange. There are also hybrids varying from creamy to salmon, some pastel, some in vivid hues. They prosper in full sun and well-drained soil.

The tawny daylily has spread so successfully on its own and with the help of admiring gardeners, the species is considered weedy by *Hemerocallis* devotees. In the right place, such as by a barn-red vacation house, it is ideal, self-reliant, and completely carefree.

Basic yellow, gold, and orange are clearly expressed in the marigolds of summer and fall. Mexican mint marigold and Copper Canyon daisy (perennial species of *Tagetes*) are glowing gold and don't appear until late fall; set next to silver leaves such as artemisia 'Powis Castle' they are most intense on a gray day. The pot-marigolds (*Calendula*) extend the show in cooler weather, which makes them popular as a winter-spring cut flower crop.

Coleus 'Fairway Yellow' and 'Pineapple Wizard' grow into knee-high bushes made up entirely of bright chartreuse and yellow leaves, with best color developing in half-day or more direct sun. *Pelargonium* 'Cloth of Gold' is one of several fancyleaf geraniums having lime-yellow foliage.

Some additional sources for yellow among annuals for summer and autumn: sulfur cosmos 'Bright Lights,' *Chrysanthemum multicaule* 'Moonlight,' *Dahlia* 'Sunny Yellow,' California poppy (*Eschscholzia*), *Gazania* 'Talent,' sunflower (*Helianthus*), *Melampodium* 'Medallion,' petunia 'Carpet Buttercream,' and many zinnias, from the profuse, small-flowered, narrow-leaf (*Z. linearis*) to the larger saucer-size 'Dreamland Yellow.'

Chrysanthemum morifolium, the florist mum—above, in a pale yellow, with slightly incurved petals that are also quilled—has been cultivated for thousands of years. There are also hardy mums that come back year after year—all in every yellow imaginable. Sulfur cosmos 'Bright Lights' (right) blooms summer-fall, ideal for the garden and cutting.

Widely adapted, *Potentilla fruticosa* becomes a woody perennial with yellow flowers all summer. Blanket-flower *Gaillardia (foreground)* can be annual or perennial, with a long season of reddish-yellow, bicolored, or red blooms.

A summer-planted, hardy bulb, *Sternbergia lutea* announces the arrival of autumn with its chrome-yellow, crocus-like flowers that sprout up almost overnight in early fall and bloom on naked stems. Since the leaves appear in spring, then disappear, a summer companion is needed, such as orange impatiens *(shown)*, or a carpeting yellow-leaved plant such as golden thyme *(Thymus)*.

'Little Aurora' hosta's lime-yellow leaves stand out in a garden even at night. Dusky violet-blue flowers appear in summer. 'Kabitan,' another small hosta, has yellow-green lance leaves with a narrow dark green edge.

'Gold Standard' hosta is one of the garden's most dramatic yellow-leaved perennials. The reverse of its color pattern is seen in 'Aurora Borealis,' whose large, quilted leaves are flamed yellow-green at the edges, highlighting the powdery, blue-green centers.

Impatiens hawkeri, a species from New Guinea, has passed its genes for golden leaves on to a generation of hybrids *(above)* with large, showy flowers and brightly variegated foliage. 'Texas Gold,' a low branching impatiens of the sultana type, has clear, golden-chartreuse leaves and pink to tangerine flowers.

he yellows and golds of summer reach a crescendo in autumn, an earthly response to the waning of the sun's rays. Dahlias, roses, and chrysanthemums stand out in these colors but it is when trees and shrubs start to turn yellow overnight—aspen, poplar, ginkgo, *Lindera obtusiloba*—that the changing of the seasons becomes official. It takes a sharp eye to spot them amongst the dying leaves, but there they are: tiny, ribbony, yellow witch hazel flowers from *Hamamelis virginiana*, possibly the latest woody plant to bloom in temperate climates.

Besides all the sources of yellow flowers and leaves mentioned specifically in these pages, here are the clues for spotting such plants in a listing of botanical names: *auratus* (golden, gold-colored); *aureo-* (prefix meaning golden); *aureus, -a, -um* (golden); *flavescens* (yellowish; becoming yellow); *flavi-* (prefix meaning yellow); *flavus, -a, -um* (yellow); *luteolus, -a, -m* (yellowish); *lutescens* (becoming yellowish); *luteus, -a, -um* (yellow).

(5)

complementary color schemes

ELLOW'S OPPOSITE ON THE COLOR WHEEL IS VIOLET, GOLD'S
(or yellow-orange's) is blue-violet, orange's is blue, and yellow-green's is
red-violet. Mixed or matched, these are highly complementary—for example yellow and orange English wallflowers *(Cheiranthus)* with blue *Myosotis* forget-me-nots
(opposite) for spring, or the same complementary colors in summer from a host of
yellow and orange daylilies *(Hemerocallis)* and blue *Aster, Campanula,* and *Veronica.*

Another approach to developing a complementary color scheme is to repeat
the colors in a single blossom, a bicolored tulip such as 'Helmar' *(above)*, for
example, a Rembrandt with red-violet feathering in a field of creamy yellow.

Yellow-and-white as a garden color scheme might be taken from any number of dahlias, from those whose deep yellow petals are merely tipped in white to those with so much white they are cream yellow. The Shasta daisy, with white rays and golden disks, is often used with pinks and blues—roses, delphiniums—but try it with lime lady's-mantle *(Alchemilla),* yellow-leaved spirea, and a golden sage *(Salvia).*

No season is without its quota of yellow and white flowers, but considering their potentially cooling effect by day, and their luminosity which can be appreciated on moonlit walks, summer seems ideal. The city terrace container garden *(right)* includes some prime players for a mating of yellow *(Coreopsis, Rudbeckia)* and white ('White Swan' *Echinacea,* white *Liatris).* The sunflowers *(Helianthus)* are a major source for yellow, and sometimes even white (the Italian). Hollyhocks *(Alcea)* come in both colors, as do achillea, *Deutzia crenata* 'Summer Snow,' yucca, honeysuckle *(Lonicera),* and jasmine *(Jasminum).*

🌱 A half-round wooden planter for a city terrace is filled with *Coreopsis verticillata* 'Moonbeam,' *Echinacea* 'White Swan,' golden-glow *(Rudbeckia laciniata* 'Hortensia'), and white *Liatris.*

🐦 Snowy, fragrant, white Dutch hyacinths and bright yellow 'Peeping Tom' daffodils *(Narcissus)* are enhanced by a dreamy go-between: white and pale yellow 'Ice Follies' daffodil.

🐦 Lemon-yellow and cherry-red tulips set the color scheme for a spring garden.

Primary yellow and red together in a garden can be cheery or even brash *(above)*. Deep yellow and harmonious shades of gold, mixed with warm reds, make for a rich effect easily gotten in spring with tulips and other bulbs, wallflower *(Cheiranthus)*, and pansy *(Viola)*, later from a host of annuals and perennials, and finally, in autumn, the hardy chrysanthemums, whose family is generously endowed in this range.

American native perennials that combine gold and red-mahogany in one flower include *Ratibida*, or Mexican-hat (there is also a form that is entirely golden yellow), blanket-flower *Gaillardia*, and numerous annual *Tagetes* of the French marigold type. These plants are widely adapted for blooms all summer.

Bright yellow lantanas, in training as tree-form standards, grow as giant lollipops from a bed of red *Begonia semperflorens*. There is also a pale yellow lantana and one whose flowers can be yellow, orange, and red all at once. Blue sage and yellow marigolds grow in the background. All bloom best in warm, frost-free weather, and sun.

The color yellow is curiously missing—or mostly so—from the always-in-bloom bedding begonia, B. *semperflorens*, yet its many shades of red, from rosy to almost orange, get on well with yellow flowers such as lantana and foliages such as gold coleus. Each blossom—if it is of the single type—has a prominent display of yellow-to-golden color at its center: scintillating clusters of pollen grains if it is the male, pronged and minutely haired receptacles if the female. A rare development from Logee's Greenhouses is double B. *semperflorens*, whose densely packed petals can be partly or entirely yellow, some pale, others sulfur-yellow. Any of these begonias can come also with green or dark red leaves, the latter flattering to yellow flowers.

Creamy yellow spires of *Baptisia* stand out in front of dark red wallflower *(Cheiranthus)*. The soft yellows can serve as accents or for blending darker and lighter shades. Later, when the baptisia has finished, the potentilla in back and hybrid lilies *(Lilium)* will add bright yellow to this part of the garden.

The drama of a red-and-yellow scheme can be heightened by the range of shades used. A pale or lemony yellow such as from a cultivar of hardy herbaceous perennial *Baptisia (left)* has the power to make the other colors appear more deeply brilliant.

By contrast, a high note expressed in a clear lipstick red, such as small-flowered but profuse and always-in-bloom *Salvia gregii* can have a magical effect in playing up the darker, more vivid yellows such as from *Coreopsis* 'Early Sunrise,' gold-and-mahogany French marigold *(Tagetes)*, and 'Crimson Pygmy' barberry *(Berberis) (opposite)*.

The yellow-and-red team also includes purple fountain grass *(Pennisetum)*, purple perilla, and 'Purple Ruffles' basil *(Ocimum)*. The herb known as bronze fennel *(Foeniculum vulgare* 'Purpureum') combines reddish leaves all season that are crowned by late summer with umbels of tiny yellow flowers.

🌱 Tulip yellow and forget-me-not blue is one of nature's most ubiquitous complementary color schemes, a floral mirror to sunbeams and blue skies. A similar effect might be gotten in summer by placing in a bed of yellow flowers a large blue-and-white ceramic pot.

Velvety bright yellow and gleaming mahogany pansies in an antique concrete urn affirm the synergy of yellow and red together, in this case a red so saturated with color it is reddish-brown.

(6)

w a r m   c l i m a t e   y e l l o w s

YELLOW'S RELATIVE COLORFASTNESS FAVORS ITS POPULARITY in warm-climate landscapes. Moreover, many plants native to the tropics have disproportionately large golden flowers, such as in selections of Chinese hibiscus *(above)*, or an extraordinary appearance, as in the yellow ladyslipper orchids *(opposite)* of noble bearing. The climbing *Solandra*, from Central America and the West Indies, is called "golden chalice" for the color and shape of its blossoms, as wide as a dinner plate. The cultivar 'Warrimoo' from *Solandra maxima* also has creamy yellow-variegated foliage. Croton *(Codiaeum)* can be a shrub or small tree with green-veined, bright yellow leaves. There is also gold *Dieffenbachia* 'Rudolf Roehrs,' yellow *Sansevieria* 'Golden Hahnii,' yellow bloodleaf *Iresine lindenii* 'Formosa,' and yellow calico plant *Alternanthera ficoidea* 'Aurea.'

🐝 Yellow oleander *(left)* is *Thevetia peruviana*, with tea-rose scented flowers any time it has sun, heat, and water. The plant is an evergreen shrub or small tree.

🌿 Hummingbirds favor the intricate yellow flowers of *Passiflora citrina (above, upper)*, from the American tropics. Golden trumpet-vine *(above, lower)* is *Allamanda cathartica* 'Hendersonii.' It can be shrubby or a huge vine.

Yellow king's-crown (*Justicia aurea*) shows off its feathery plumes in warm weather, seen at right against a background of shoulder-high 'Blue African' basil (*Ocimum*). Justicia can be cut back and carried through winter in a moderately warm, frost-free place.

Yellow shrimp plant, *Justicia brandegeana* 'Lutea,' has long-lasting lemon-yellow bracts from which the ephemeral white flowers are borne. In the related *Pachystachys lutea*, or lollipop plant, the bracts are held decidedly upright and they are a richer, golden yellow that almost glows.

Columnea, a genus of upright or trailing gesneriads, includes several yellows that bloom constantly in warm, moist, brightness, outdoors or in, such as 'Top Brass' and 'Yellow Dragon.'

The yellow calla lily, *Zantedeschia elliottiana*, is a regal flower for growing in summer pots or beds. During this active time the tuberous roots need a constant supply of water—pots may be left standing in it—but in winter they can be kept nearly dry and in the dark.

The orchid family glitters with gold among the butterfly and dancing-lady yellows in the genus *Oncidium* (*right, upper*). *Anguloa clowesii*, the tulip orchid, is bright yellow, and so too the tulip cattleya, *C. citrina*, and many different species of *Dendrobium*.

Yellow-flowered trees can be prominent in mild-climate gardens, such as the fragrant *Acacia* (*right, lower*), golden-bell *Tabebuia argentea*, golden trumpet-tree *T. chrysotricha*, and ylang-ylang (*Cananga odorata*) with ribbony yellow flowers treasured for their sweet-smelling perfume.

Two members of the pea family, *Cassia* and *Senna*, contain showy yellow-flowering shrubs and trees. While many are for warm climates, wild senna (*S. marilandica*) blooms gold in summer everywhere.

Notable yellow-flowered vines for warm gardens include *Merremia tuberosa* (wood-rose), *Hibbertia scandens* (gold-vine), and *Stigmaphyllon ciliatum* with frilly blooms followed by showy, butterfly-shaped green seeds.

Dancing lady and butterfly orchids *(Oncidium)* bloom yellow over a long season *(above)*.

Acacia contains a host of arid, warm-climate trees *(below)* and shrubs, outstanding for their yellow, unique perfume, and the florist cut flower called "mimosa."

sources

Jacques Amand
P.O. Box 59001
Potomac, MD 20859
free catalog; all kinds of bulbs

Amaryllis, Inc.
P.O. Box 318
Baton Rouge, LA 70821
free list; hybrid Hippeastrum

Antique Rose Emporium
Rt. 5, Box 143
Brenham, TX 77833
*catalog $5; old roses; also
perennials, ornamental grasses*

B & D Lilies
330 "P" Street
Port Townsend, WA 98368
catalog $3; garden lilies

Kurt Bluemel
2740 Greene Lane
Baldwin, MD 21013
*catalog $2; ornamental grasses;
perennials*

Bluestone Perennials
7237 Middle Ridge
Madison, OH 44057
free catalog; perennials

Borboleta Gardens
15980 Canby Avenue, Rt. 5
Faribault, MN 55021
*catalog $3; bulbs, tubers, corms,
rhizomes*

Brand Peony Farms
P.O. Box 842
St. Cloud, MN 56302
free catalog; peonies

Breck's
6523 N. Galena Road
Peoria, IL 61632
free catalog; all kinds of bulbs

Briarwood Gardens
14 Gully Lane, R.F.D. 1
East Sandwich, MA 02537
list $1; azaleas, rhododendrons

W. Atlee Burpee Co.
300 Park Avenue
Warminster, PA 18974
*free catalog; seeds, plants, bulbs,
supplies; wide selection*

Busse Gardens
5873 Oliver Avenue S.W.
Cokato, MN 55321
catalog $2; perennials

Canyon Creek Nursery
3527 Dry Creek Road
Oroville, CA 95965
catalog $2; silver-leaved plants

Carroll Gardens
Box 310
Westminster, MD 21158
*catalog $2; perennials, woodies,
herbs*

Coastal Gardens
4611 Socastee Boulevard
Myrtle Beach, SC 29575
catalog $3; perennials

The Cummins Garden
22 Robertsville Road
Marlboro, NJ 07746
*catalog $2; azaleas,
rhododendrons, woodies*

Daylily World
P.O. Box 1612
Sanford, FL 32772
*catalog $5; all kinds of
hemerocallis*

deJager Bulb Co.
Box 2010
South Hamilton, MA 01982
free list; all kinds of bulbs

Tom Dodd's Rare Plants
9131 Holly Street
Semmes, AL 36575
*list $1; trees, shrubs, extremely
select*

Far North Gardens
16785 Harrison Road
Livonia, MI 48154
*catalog $2; primulas, other
perennials*

Howard B. French
Box 565
Pittsfield, VT 05762
free catalog; bulbs

Gardens of the Blue Ridge
Box 10
Pineola, NC 28662
catalog $3; wildflowers and ferns

D.S. George Nurseries
2515 Penfield Road
Fairport, NY 14450
free catalog; clematis

**Glasshouse Works
Greenhouses**
Church Street, Box 97
Stewart, OH 45778
catalog $2; exotics for containers

Greenlee Ornamental Grasses
301 E. Franklin Avenue
Pomona, CA 91766
catalog $5; native and ornamental grasses

Greer Gardens
1280 Goodpasture Is. Rd.
Eugene, OR 97401
catalog $3; uncommon woodies, especially rhododendrons

Grigsby Cactus Gardens
2354 Bella Vista Drive
Vista, CA 92084
catalog $2; cacti and other succulents

Growers Service Co.
10118 Crouse Road
Hartland, MI 48353
list $1; all kinds of bulbs

Heirloom Old Garden Roses
24062 N.E. Riverside Drive
St. Paul, OR 97137
catalog $5; old garden, English, and winter-hardy roses

J.L. Hudson, Seedsman
P.O. Box 1058
Redwood City, CA 94064
catalog $1; nonhybrid flowers, vegetables

Jackson and Perkins
1 Rose Lane
Medford, OR 97501
free catalog; roses, perennials

Kartuz Greenhouses
1408 Sunset Drive
Vista, CA 92083
catalog $2; exotics for containers

Klehm Nursery
Rt. 5, Box 197
Penny Road
South Barrington, IL 60010
catalog $5; peonies, hemerocallis, hostas, perennials

M. & J. Kristick
155 Mockingbird Road
Wellsville, PA 17365
free catalog; conifers

Lamb Nurseries
Rt. 1, Box 460B
Long Beach, WA 98631
catalog $1; perennials

Lauray of Salisbury
432 Undermountain Road,
Rt. 41
Salisbury, CT 06068
catalog $2; exotics for containers

Lilypons Water Gardens
6800 Lilypons Road
P.O. Box 10
Buckeystown, MD 21717
catalog $5; aquatics

Limerock Ornamental Grasses
R.D. 1, Box 111
Port Matilda, PA 16870
list $3

Logee's Greenhouses
141 North Street
Danielson, CT 06239
catalog $3; exotics for containers

Louisiana Nursery
Rt. 7, Box 43
Opelousas, LA 70570
catalogs $3-$6; uncommon woodies, perennials

Lowe's Own Root Roses
6 Sheffield Road
Nashua, NH 03062
list $5; old roses

McClure & Zimmerman
Box 368
Friesland, WI 53935
free catalog; all kinds of bulbs

Merry Gardens
Upper Mechanic Street,
Box 595
Camden, ME 04843
catalog $2; herbs, Pelargoniums, cultivars of Hedera helix

Milaeger's Gardens
4838 Douglas Avenue
Racine, WI 53402
catalog $1; perennials

Moore Miniature Roses
2519 E. Noble Avenue
Visalia, CA 93292
catalog $1; all kinds of miniature roses

Niche Gardens
1111 Dawson Road
Chapel Hill, NC 27516
catalog $3; perennials

Nor'East Miniature Roses
Box 307
Rowley, MA 01969
free catalog

Oakes Daylilies
8204 Monday Road
Corryton, TN 37721
free catalog; all kinds of hemerocallis

Geo. W. Park Seed Co.
Box 31
Greenwood, SC 29747
free catalog; all kinds of seeds, plants, and bulbs

Roses of Yesterday and Today
802 Brown's Valley Road
Watsonville, CA 95076
catalog $3 third class, $5 first; old roses

Seymour's Selected Seeds
P.O. Box 1346
Sussex, VA 23884
free catalog; English cottage garden seeds

Shady Hill Gardens
821 Walnut Street
Batavia, IL 60510
catalog $2; 800 different Pelargonium

Shady Oaks Nursery
112 10th Ave. S.E.
Waseca, MN 56093
catalog $2.50; hostas, ferns, wildflowers, shrubs

Siskiyou Rare Plant Nursery
2825 Cummings Road
Medford, OR 97501
catalog $2; alpines

Anthony J. Skittone
1415 Eucalyptus
San Francisco, CA 94132
catalog $2; unusual bulbs, especially from South Africa

Sonoma Horticultural Nursery
3970 Azalea Avenue
Sebastopol, CA 95472
catalog $2; azaleas, rhododendrons

Spring Hill Nurseries
110 W. Elm Street
Tipp City, OH 45371
free catalog; perennials, woodies, roses

Steffen Nurseries
Box 184
Fairport, NY 14450
catalog $2; clematis

Sunnybrook Farms Homestead
9448 Mayfield Road
Chesterland, OH 44026
catalog $2; perennials, herbs

Surry Gardens
P.O. Box 145
Surry, ME 04684
free list; perennials, vines, grasses, wild garden

Thompson & Morgan
Box 1308
Jackson, NJ 08527
free catalog; all kinds of seeds

Transplant Nursery
1586 Parkertown Road
Lavonia, GA 30553
catalog $1; azaleas, rhododendrons

Van Engelen, Inc.
Stillbrook Farm
313 Maple Street
Litchfield, CT 06759
free catalog; all kinds of bulbs

Andre Viette Farm & Nursery
Rt. 1, Box 16
Fishersville, VA 22939
catalog $3; perennials, ornamental grasses

Washington Evergreen Nursery
Box 388
Leicester, NC 28748
catalog $2; conifers

Wayside Gardens
One Garden Lane
Hodges, SC 29695
free catalog; all kinds of bulbs, woodies, perennials, vines

We-Du Nursery
Rt. 5, Box 724
Marion, NC 28752
catalog $2; uncommon woodies, perennials

White Flower Farm
Box 50
Litchfield, CT 06759
catalog $5; woodies, perennials, bulbs

Gilbert H. Wild and Son, Inc.
Sarcoxie, MO 64862
catalog $3; perennials, peonies, iris, hemerocallis

Yucca Do
P.O. Box 655
Waller, TX 77484
catalog $2; woodies, perennials

index